"Sister Sandra DeGidio's little book provides some very practical tips and useful texts to make any visit to the infirm or homebound a much more prayerful experience. The rapidly growing number of people who regularly call upon the sick should welcome this resource with open arms."

Rev. Joseph A. Champlin, Author
A Thoughtful Word, A Healing Touch

"For some time, now, thank God, spiritual care of the sick has been seen as the obligation of the entire parish, and this book offers parish ministers to the sick simple, sensitive prayers with corresponding readings from Scripture. The author has identified nineteen pastoral situations and needs that a visitor is likely to encounter, including cancer, heart disease, stroke, loss of a premature newborn, and impending surgery. This is a valuable addition to parish and pastoral care department resource shelves."

Margot Hover
Healthcare Chaplaincy
Memorial Sloan-Kettering Cancer Center

"Often those visiting the sick are performing a ministry that is much needed, but they may not be as comfortable with 'closeness' as they ought to be. This work eases the way for virtually anyone to be an effective servant of healing and/or consolation. Because this book gives specific situations as well as instructions for the caregiver, it allows and assists the person to get close and serve as a true healer and caregiver for the person being visited."

Richard A. Kirsch
Director of Continuing Education
Sacred Heart School of Theology

"Once again Sister Sandra DeGidio supports and encourages the caregivers of the world through this thoughtful book. Her beautiful from-the-heart prayers accentuate Jesus' lifelong ministry to ease the person in distress. Beginners in the ministry will find the 'tips for visiting the sick' very apropos."

Sister Diane Traffas
Catholic Health Initiatives
Upper Midwest Region

"This slim volume fits easily into a pocket, briefcase, or handbag, and certainly into one's heart. It contains prayers and scriptural selections that link the patient's condition to Christ's suffering and salvation to foster a spirit of peace and comfort during the visit."

Patti Normile
Author, *Visiting the Sick: A Guide for Parish Ministers,*
Prayers for Caregivers

"This is an easy-to-use primer of prayer suggestions for those who visit and care for the sick. It will be especially helpful to those new to the ministry of healing who are looking for fresh ways to pray with and comfort the sick. By providing these short prayers and Scripture readings for a variety of circumstances, Sr. Sandra hopes to promote creativity and sensitivity in how we share faith and prayer in our healing ministry."

Rev. Gerard Broccolo, STD, Vice President
Spirituality of Catholic Health Initiatives

Sandra DeGidio, OSM

PRAYING
WITH THE
SICK

- Prayers
- Services
- Rituals

XXIII

TWENTY-THIRD PUBLICATIONS

Mystic, CT 06355

Twenty-Third Publications
185 Willow Street
P.O. Box 180
Mystic, CT 06355
(860) 536-2611
800-321-0411

ISBN 0-89622-893-2
Library of Congress Catalog Card Number 97-62068
Printed in the U.S.A.

Dedication

To Bonnie Alho, OSM

who encouraged, coaxed, cheered,

and wanted this book more than anyone

Contents

Part Four

Scripture Readings to Accompany
  Specific Prayers
*Note that for ease of use in finding them, these readings
bear the same titles as the prayers in Part Three.*

PRAYING WITH THE SICK

Introduction

Picture it.....

The Time:

A bright, warm Sunday morning in June of 1987.

The Place: A hospital room in a large Midwestern city.

In the room are two women who had each had major surgery a few days before. One was Catholic, the other was not.

Earlier that morning, both women had been freed of their IVs and NG tubes. Delighted with their new-found freedom, they were visiting through the privacy curtain between their beds.

While they were chatting, there was a knock on the door. Without waiting for a response a woman pushed open the door, and without looking directly at the patient in the first bed inside the room, or acknowledging the conversation in progress, said, "Hello, I have communion for you." Then, barely taking a breath, she began reciting the Lord's Prayer.

The woman in the second bed, unaware of what was happening on the other side of the curtain, continued talking. The rather astonished woman in the first bed, who should have been praying with the communion distributor, said to her roommate, "Uh, excuse me, there's someone here with communion for me, would you like to pray with us?" The roommate stopped talking abruptly. The hospital visitor kept right on praying.

Following the Lord's Prayer, the woman pulled a folded white cloth from the pocket of her dress, opened it, removed a host, said, "Body of Christ," placed the host in the hand of the somewhat startled patient, stood there for a few moments while the host was being consumed, and then, still not looking directly at the woman to whom she was ministering, said "Well, goodbye, hope you get well soon."

As Dave Barry is wont to say, I'm not making this up. I was the recipient of that curious communion call.

I felt for my visitor. She seemed so uncomfortable, so unsure of what to say or do except the most minimal and rubrical. After she left, I was tempted to call the hospital chaplain's office and offer an intensive on-site training session for their volunteer visitors. After all, the doctor had just told me I would be there three more days and I had experience visiting the sick and had helped prepare others to do the same.

Since that bright, warm Sunday morning in 1987, there have been numerous changes in both health care delivery and pastoral care of the sick.

Hospital stays are much shorter than they were ten

years ago. People are sicker at home. They are often overwhelmed, fearful, and anxious about their recovery. In addition, our aging population means that there are more homebound older adults who are regularly visited, often by volunteer parish visitors and/or eucharistic ministers.

Hospice, the program designed to provide a physically and emotionally caring environment for the terminally ill, has grown significantly in the last ten years. Visitors of the sick are now regularly called upon to also provide spiritual care to hospice residents and their families.

Those who visit the sick—professional chaplains or pastoral ministers, as well as volunteer parish visitors and parish nurses—are much better prepared for their ministry. They understand the importance of being truly present to the person they're visiting. They are aware of the art of compassionate conversation and active listening. They are also aware of the power of physical touch and the healing effect of tears.

In light of those changes, I offer this little book as a gift to all of you entrusted with the healing ministry of visiting the sick and shut-ins. It is my hope that it will assist you in your ministry and help enhance and personalize your prayer with those you visit.

Part One

When Visiting the Sick

In their book *A Thoughtful Word, A Healing Touch* (Twenty-Third Publications) Father Joe Champlin and Susan Champlin Taylor list "Ten Useful Tips for Visiting the Sick." While most of you who are using this book are probably aware of these valuable tips, they are worth repeating. With permission from Twenty-Third Publications I include them here, and add five of my own.

1. Be there.

The first step is to realize that it is your presence, not your words, that means the most. Remember, there is no magic formula, there are no magic words. Just being present for that moment will go a long way toward helping the person heal, if not physically, then at least emotionally.

2. Know the power of touch.

Holding a person's hand or giving a comforting pat on the arm can mean a great deal to someone fighting fear and loneliness. Naturally, it depends on your closeness to the person and on his or her willingness to be touched, but a visitor who stays at arm's length from the patient may be unconsciously exacerbating the sense of separation that a seriously ill person already feels. A gentle touch tells the person you're willing to be *with* them.

3. Listen.

Come to the visit with an open agenda. Let the patient lead in telling you what his or her needs are. If he or she wants to recount favorite stories—even if you've heard them several times before—listening with enthusiasm can validate the person's sense of self-worth.

4. You don't need the "right" answers.

A person confronted with a life-threatening [or any other illness] often asks, "Why me?" Many visitors feel they are supposed to have an answer, one that will make the patient "feel better." But the familiar clichés one uses to make sense of the tragedy ("It's part of God's plan." "Everything happens for a reason.") can sometimes do more harm than good. The ill person frequently isn't really looking for an answer but is expressing his or her confusion. So the best thing to do is to repeat the question in your own words, indicating that you understand the person's anxiety. "I see you're really troubled by this" is a more helpful response than "God is testing you."

5. *Validate the person's emotions.*

Too often, because of our own discomfort, we try to avoid the subject of illness or death and don't allow patients to discuss their feelings. If they say, "I know I'm not getting better," responding with "Don't talk that way" does not help them come to grips with the situation. Instead of suggesting that they keep their feelings to themselves, encourage them to express their fear or concerns; this way they know that you're willing to journey with them, and that you understand their thoughts and emotions.

6. *Don't be afraid of tears.*

Again, saying to a person, "Don't cry," is more hurtful than it is helpful. Tears help heal, and bottling up one's emotions is unhealthy. You don't have to say anything; you can just hold the person's hand. And don't be afraid of your own tears. Let them flow.

7. *Try to be compassionate.*

We can be better prepared to handle a patient's emotions if we know something about what he or she is experiencing. Terminal patients in particular experience a variety of moods and emotions, among them anger, depression, denial, false hope, peace, and acceptance. There is no one formula for how and when they will experience these, but these emotions are common among the seriously ill. Try to be open to wherever they are at any given time so that you can respond with understanding and compassion.

Keep in mind, too, that anger and frustration may sometimes be directed toward loved ones. Visitors need to realize that this is not personal, but part of the response to the illness. Also, not every sick person experiences peace and/or acceptance. However, your visits will go a long way toward helping the person reach this goal if you are able to offer compassion, love, and acceptance.

8. Monitor what you say.

Even if patients are unconscious or seem unaware of what's going on around them, they may be able to hear what is said to them. Thus visitors should not only guard against saying negative things, but should continue to express words of love and encouragement.

9. Keep your visit brief.

Seriously ill people tire easily but may feel obliged to put on a good face for visitors. Frequent brief visits are better than infrequent long ones. Find out the best time to visit, and plan your call accordingly.

10. Be yourself.

If you have always been an optimistic, upbeat person and carry that tone naturally into the sickroom with you, fine. But trying to put on a show of cheerful-

ness when you don't feel it will immediately strike a
false note the patient will detect. Don't put pressure on
yourself by feeling you have to "accomplish" something during the visit. You're there just to provide support, which the patient will appreciate more than any
platitudes or jokes you may offer. As one hospice
director says, "Remember, anything is the right thing
to say as long as you're sincere."*

11. Ask what the person would like to pray about.

Don't assume that you know what is the best prayer
for the patient. Ask what they might like to pray for
and be open and flexible to their request. When people are very ill or in great pain, they are often unable
to pray. If, however, they do choose to initiate the
prayer, follow their lead. You can always add to the
prayer or conclude with a blessing of the person. Also,
be sure that the person is aware of the precise nature of
the illness before using a specific prayer (for example,
the "Prayer for Someone with Cancer").

12. Sometimes the visit is the prayer.

I once made regular "communion call" visits to an
elderly woman who was well enough to care for her-
self, but because of limited mobility was pretty much

*A Thoughtful Word, A Healing Touch by Rev. Joseph Champlin and
Susan Champlin Taylor is published by Twenty-Third Publications, P.O.
Box 180, Mystic, CT 06355, 800-321-0411.

homebound. She always knew when I was coming and would bake for my arrival. Inevitably her first words as I'd come in the door were, "Let's get communion over with so we can eat." For her, the prayer–the communion–included the time spent visiting over her baked goods and coffee.

13. *If possible, include the family in the prayer.*
When family members are present with the sick person, invite them to participate in the prayer. They might read a Scripture passage, pray a favorite psalm, offer spontaneous or traditional prayers. Also integrate them into the prayer, mentioning them by name or relationship, whether or not they are physically present. Doing so can be comforting for both patient and family.

14. *Use symbols.*
The sick and shut-ins often feel isolated from their worshiping community. To help unite the person with the community, a nice practice is to bring them cut flowers or plants that have been in the sanctuary during Mass. During major feasts of the liturgical year, share symbols of the season: ashes, palms, Easter water, a purple candle to light during Advent, a tape of the community singing Christmas hymns or the Easter Alleluia, etc.

15. *Use healing music.*

For some visits, especially to hospice or the person's home, bring healing music. Carry a small tape recorder with calming harp, flute, violin, or other music to accompany your visit and prayer. Such CDs and tapes are readily available these days.

Part Two

How To Use This Book

The prayers for specific needs and illnesses in this book (see Part Three), are designed to be incorporated into a basic "Prayer Service Format," as on pages 13 and 14. Please feel free to adapt the order of this service according to the needs and desires of the person with whom you are visiting and praying.

When visiting the sick, flexibility is extremely important. However, it is equally important to be prepared.

In preparation for your visit then, choose the prayer appropriate to the illness from Part Three. Have several Scripture readings chosen and marked in your Bible. A "suggested" reading is listed at the end of each prayer and these are also printed in full in Part Four of this book. Feel free, however, to choose whichever readings best fit you and the person you are visiting. Or the person you're visiting may have a favorite Scripture passage they would like used.

When visiting on a Sunday, use one or more of the readings of the day. If the person is very ill or weak, you may want to use just a verse or two of the gospel reading. This will help the person feel a connection with the worshiping community. In all cases, be open to the needs and desires of the patient.

If the person you are visiting is very ill (e.g., a stroke or coma victim unable to speak or a person near death), you may want to simply spend a short amount of time comforting and talking to the patient, then say a prayer related to the person's illness and give them a blessing. If the person is going into surgery or has a terminal illness, a more detailed service with Scripture readings might be beneficial.

As already mentioned, it is important to know the condition and needs of the person you are visiting. On arrival, introduce yourself. Initiate conversation about the person's illness. Let patients tell you about how they feel physically and emotionally. Validate their feelings. Ask if they would like to pray and if there is anything special they would like to pray about or if there is a particular prayer or Scripture reading they would like to pray. Before beginning the prayer, ask if the patient and/or family members would like to receive communion. Don't just assume that they would.

Prayer Service Format

Greeting
Hello, I'm N. from St. N. Parish. I've come to visit and pray with you. Is this a good time? How are you feeling today?...

Sign of the Cross

Opening Prayer
Lord Jesus Christ, you cured the bodies, nursed the souls, and healed the hearts of all the sick who came to you in faith. We come to you in faith today and ask that you touch N. with your healing power. Amen.

Scripture Reading (See Part Four)

Shared or Silent Meditation/Reflection
(Spend a few minutes in silence or sharing together how the Scripture reading touches or speaks to you.)

Penitential Prayer
To prepare for communion, let us pause for a moment to be aware of God's presence and to renew our sorrow for our sins. (Pray together an act of contrition, or the following, or a similar litany of contrition.)

Loving God, you are with us and for us:
Lord, have mercy.

Compassionate Christ, you give strength to the
    weak and weary:
Christ, have mercy.
Healing Jesus, you have the power to heal our over-
    burdened bodies and souls:
Lord, have mercy.

Lord's Prayer
Let us praise God's goodness and compassion, even in
our illness by praying together the prayer Jesus taught
us. Our Father...

Communion
This is the Lamb of God who takes away the sin of the
world, who comforts, heals, and strengthens. Happy
are those called to his supper.

Closing Prayer
(See Part Three for a prayer appropriate to the illness
or situation.)

Blessing
*While tracing a Sign of the Cross on the forehead of the
patient:*

May the God of comfort and compassion be with
you in your time of illness (trial) and give you light,
peace, and consolation. Amen.

Alternate Blessings

You may want to use one of the following blessings in place of or in addition to the blessing on page 14.

May God give you light and peace. Amen.
May God give you courage and strength. Amen.
May God raise you up and save you. Amen.
And may Almighty God bless you in the name of the
Father, and of the Son, and of the Holy Spirit. Amen.

May our Lord Jesus Christ,
who went about doing good and healing the sick
grant you restored health
and may you be enriched by his blessings. Amen.

May our all-loving God
touch you with healing power and strength. Amen.
May God bless you,
give health to your body,
holy strength to your soul,
and bring you safely to eternal life. Amen.

(For One Near Death)
May God be with you to protect you. Amen.
May Christ go before you to guide you
and stand beside you to give you strength. Amen.
May the Holy Spirit embrace you and lead you safely
to the kingdom of light and eternal life. Amen.

Part Three

Prayers for Specific Situations

The first two prayers in this section are general healing prayers and can be used with anyone you might be visiting. Thereafter, the prayers are more specific.

Prayer to Christ the Healer

In the comfort of your love,
I pour out to you, my Savior,
the memories that haunt me,
the anxieties that perplex me,
the fears that stifle me,
the sickness that prevails upon me,
and the frustration of all
the pain that weaves about within me.
Lord, help me to see
your peace in my turmoil,
your compassion in my sorrow,
your forgiveness in my weakness,
and your love in my need.
Touch me, O Lord, with your
healing power and strength.

(© Alexian Brothers)

Litany of Christ the Healer

Lord Jesus, Son of God and our brother,
>	heal and save us.
Lord Jesus, you bore our ills
>	and carried our griefs,
>	heal and save us.
Lord Jesus, you preached Good News
and raised up those with illness and disease,
>	heal and save us.
Lord Jesus, you touched the woman bent double
and she stood straight;
you let yourself be touched by the
hemorrhaging woman
and she was cured,
>	heal and save us.
Lord Jesus, you restored sight to the blind
and hope to the downhearted,
>	heal and save us.
Lord Jesus, you cured Peter's mother-in-law,
>	Jairus' daughter,
>		the only son of the widow of Nain,
>		the centurion's servant,
>		heal and save us.
Lord Jesus, you cast out demons
and relieved the tormented and anxious,

heal and save us.
Lord Jesus, you healed crippled limbs
and purified the skin of lepers,
    heal and save us.
Lord Jesus, you laid hands on the sick
and anointed them with the oil of gladness,
    heal and save us.
Lord Jesus, your servant N. is sick
    heal and save her/him. Amen.

For Someone Who Is Anxious or Afraid

Merciful God,
your friend N. has just received news of [name the mal-
    ady].
This announcement has made her/him anxious and
    fearful.
You know how difficult it is for us to try to accept
our afflictions, with some sort of submission,
when they actually arrive.
But Jesus' prayer to you at Gethsemane
shows that even he experienced fear and anxiety,
and the servant is not greater than the master.
N. has had challenges before,
but this one seems overpowering.
Be with her/him in this trying time.
Watch and wait with her/him.

With you, N. can survive this situation.
Her/his hope and faith in your support
will see her/him through.
Help her/him remember that
on the other side of pain lies strength,
on the other side of doubt is faith,
and on the other side of fear is love.
Merciful God,
help N. hear your voice that says be not afraid,
I'll catch you if you fall.
Let this cup of fear and anxiety pass from her/him
and give her/him peace.
In Jesus' name, we pray. Amen.
Related Scripture Reading: Matthew 8:23–27

On the Occasion of a Sudden, Unexpected Illness or Accident

God of all consolation,
your sacrament of pain and suffering
has burst suddenly into N.'s life.
May she/he accept this *(name the illness or accident)*
as part of the mystery of life and
as an opportunity to follow in the footsteps
of the Suffering Savior and his Sorrowful Mother.
We ask that this pain
not be an occasion of bitterness,

but have special meaning for her/him,
and help effect healing of body and soul.
N., may you be blessed with strength
in knowledge that in this time of pain
you are joined to Christ in his suffering
and called to be numbered among his chosen ones.
 Amen.
Related Scripture Reading: Romans 8:14–18

For Someone Going into Surgery

God of health and wholeness,
your servant N. lies here sick,
in need of surgery for _____.
Anxieties haunt her/him.
With abounding hope and faith,
we place our trust in you
and call upon the healing touch of God's grace.
We also place our trust and hope
in the hands of those
who will perform the surgery
and administer the healing medicine.
Strengthen the doctors and nurses
who will assist in this surgery.
Give them wisdom and skill,
patience and determination,
compassion and sympathy,

that they may work to cure,
speak to soothe,
and touch to heal in the power of the Holy Spirit.
    Amen.
Related Scripture Reading: Luke 7:18–22

Suggest to the person that as they go into surgery and experience the effects of the anesthetic, they visualize themselves wrapped from head to toe in a cocoon of love—love of God, family, friends, and all who care about them.

For Someone Recovering from Surgery

Compassionate God, we are deeply concerned for our friend N. Our greatest wish is that she/he might soon return to restored health.
    Lord hear our prayer.
Our prayer rises from the bottom of our hearts to you the Lord of healing and wholeness.
    Lord hear our prayer.
We know that you do not rejoice in the suffering of your people. Hear our prayer that N. may soon be pain-free and strong again.
    Lord hear our prayer.
Divine Healer, may the medicine that has been pre-scribed for N. and the care given her/him heal and call forth the hidden powers of her/his body. Through the

power of the Cross of Christ, may this medicine, blended with faith, return her/him to the fullness of health.

Lord hear our prayer.

We place in your healing hands, Merciful God, our friend N. Speed the happy day of recovery and make her/him vigorous again.

Lord hear our prayer.

We gather our prayers and offer them to God in the words that Jesus taught us. Our Father...

Related Scripture Reading: Psalm 116:1–9, 12–13

For Someone with Cancer

Loving God,
when the dreaded words *(name the specific cancer)*
are uttered,
it strikes like a sword in the heart.
Your servant N. has been struck with such a sword.
May the memory of the swords
that pierced the heart of Mary
at the prophecy of Simeon
be a consolation at this time.
Be near N. in this time of trial, weakness, and pain.
Sustain her/him with strength and courage
as she/he endures the needed therapy for this disease.
May peace, grace, and love surround her/him.

May the awareness of your Divine Presence
be like a tent over her/his bed of pain and suffering.
Give her/him a prayerful gratitude for her/his care.
Blessed are you, Loving God,
who rescue those you love
from pain and sickness,
heal and save your loved ones.
St. Peregrine, patron of those suffering from cancer,
Pray for N. Amen.
Related Scripture Reading: Psalm 130:1–7

For Someone with Heart Disease

Loving God,
Our friend N. is suffering from disease of the heart,
the organ which you have filled with so much love.
We thank you that this disease has not diminished the
love N. holds in her/his heart for you,
family, and friends.
At the same time, we ask that you hear our prayer
for the healing of her/him whom we love.
We know that you love N., too.
Remove this illness from her/him
so that, recovered and restored to health,
she/he may return, energized and renewed,
to the daily life that we share,
and to service to you and your people.

Place your hand on the heart of the patient.

N., may you be blessed
with the healing power and love of God
and the affection of those who love you. Amen.
Related Scripture Reading: 1 John 4:7, 11–13, 16

For a Stroke Victim

Divine Healer, God of Wholeness,
we place your servant N. in your hands.
We ask for healing of those parts of her/his body
that have been affected by the stroke she/he suffered.
We ask for healing
and also for acceptance of your holy plan
in her/his recovery.
Help her/him in the acceptance of this illness.
Support her/him with the strength of your Spirit
as she/he undergoes needed therapy,
and may that treatment
and the loving care of the therapists
stir the hidden healing powers of her/his body.

Trace the Sign of the Cross on the patient's forehead.

N., may you be blessed with the healing power
and love of God

and the affection of those who love you. Amen.
Related Scripture Reading: 1 Thessalonians 5:23–24

For Someone in Constant Pain

Lord Jesus Christ,
by your patience in suffering
you sanctified bodily pain
and gave us the example of obedience to God's will.
Be near N. in her/his pain and weakness.
Sustain her/him with your grace,
that she/he may bear the burden of pain.
Support her/him with the strength
and courage of your Spirit
that she/he may tolerate this suffering.
Fill her/his life with a sense of joy
in spite of the endless pain.
With faith and hope we pray for healing
according to your will.

Place your hand on the head of the person
or on the locus of the pain.

N., May peace, grace and love surround you,
and may the awareness
of God's compassionate presence
be a tent over your bed of pain. Amen.

Related Scripture Reading: Romans 8:18, 22–27

For Someone with a Terminal or Lingering Illness

Divine Healer, God of Wholeness,
we place N. in your hands.
We ask for healing,
but also for acceptance of this illness
and of your holy plan.
Help N., and us,
to embrace whatever you have in mind for her/him.
Support her/him in the anxieties, fears, pains
and frustrations of this illness.
Support her/him with the strength of your Holy Spirit.
We ask this in the name of Jesus,
compassionate healer of those in need of health and
hope.
Amen.

Trace the Sign of the Cross on the person's forehead and invite others in the room to do the same or choose one of the alternate blessings, pp. 15-16.

N., may you be blessed with the healing power of God
and the love of those who care about you. Amen.
Related Scripture Reading: Psalm 102:1–7, 11–12, 24

For Someone in a Coma

Place your right hand on the hand or forehead of the patient. Others in the room may also lay hands on the patient.

Compassionate God of health and wholeness,
we don't know if your servant N. can hear us
or feel our loving touch.
But we do know that you hear us.
We trust in your healing touch
and in your Divine Power
to stir the hidden healing abilities
of the human mind and body.
We pray that these God-given powers
blended with modern-day medicine
might restore physical and mental health to N.,
so that fully recovered she/he may return
with renewed zest to the daily life that we share.

While tracing a Sign of the Cross on the patient's forehead,

May you be blessed
with the healing power and love of God,
and the affection of us who also love you.
Amen.
Related Scripture Reading: Psalm 23

(The patient may also be signed by others who are in the room and, if appropriate, may also be kissed.)

For Sick Children

Lord Jesus, you called little children to yourself.
You loved them and chose to see them
    holy, happy and healthy.
N. needs your healing care now for (name the illness).
Be with her/him in this illness.
We ask this in the name of God our Creator
and the Spirit who gives life. Amen.

Trace the Sign of the Cross on the child's forehead and invite others in the room to do the same.

Loving God, bless N. with your healing presence.
    Amen.
Related Scripture Reading: Mark 10:13–16

Blessing for a Premature Newborn

God of all creation,
you continually surprise us with new creations.
Today, we celebrate the birth of N.,

this new creation in our midst.
This tiny baby mirrors your Divine Image
and we praise you for her/him.
N., we rejoice in your presence.
You are a gift and blessing to us.
We thank the Spirit who, with your parents' love,
co-created and sent you to us.
May you and your parents
be surrounded with steadfast, unconditional love.
May you know much joy in your life,
and experience the physical, mental,
emotional, and spiritual freedom
to become the individual you were created to be.
    Amen.
Related Scripture Reading: Luke 18:15–17

Parents and all present may trace the Sign of the Cross on the child's forehead and pray a personal prayer of blessing.

For Someone Who Has Lost a Baby

God of Life and Death,
we come to you today in sadness and anger
over the loss of a new life.
N. & N. *(names of parents)*

were so looking forward to this new baby
and now there is an emptiness
in their hearts and in their arms.
A very part of their own lives has died
in the death of their child.
In our inability to answer why
such a joyous beginning could not come to fullness,
we come to you, Gracious God.
Help us to go on.
Be with us
as we struggle to nurture and affirm
the lives that already exist and depend on us.
Help us to support and embrace them in our love.
Bless N. & N. *(names of parents)* in their sorrow.
Heal them of their brokenness.
Strengthen them with new energy
as they gather their lives again
and with you continue to bring new life to the world.
   Amen.
Related Scripture Reading: Jeremiah 1:4–5

For Someone Unable to Receive Communion

Divine Healer, God of Wholeness,
together we place N. in your hands.
We ask for healing.

We also ask for acceptance
of the added suffering she/he feels
because this illness makes it impossible
to receive your Son in communion.
In this sadness, we invoke the supportive spirit
of St. Juliana Falconieri, who on her deathbed
suffered the same pain and sadness.
N., may you be blessed with the love of God
and the affection of those who love you.
May the power of that communion of love
be a consolation to you.
May the power of the Divine Healer,
the healing hands of doctors and nurses,
and the prayer of those who love you
soon make your body whole,
so you may once again receive
the Body of Christ.
We ask this in the name of Jesus, the Bread of Life.
	Amen.
Related Scripture Reading: Psalm 42:1–5

For a Person Suffering from Addiction or Substance Abuse

God of Mercy,
we bless you in the name of your Son, Jesus Christ,
who ministered to all who came to him

afflicted with personal demons.
Give strength to your servant N.,
bound by the chains of addiction.
Enfold her/him in your love
and restore her/him to the freedom of God's children.
Look with compassion on all those
who have lost their health and freedom.
Restore to them the assurance of your unfailing mercy,
and strengthen them in the work of recovery.
To those who care for them,
grant patient understanding and a love that perseveres.

Now pray the Serenity Prayer with the addicted person:

God,
Grant me the serenity
     to accept the things I cannot change,
The courage to change the things I can,
And the wisdom to know the difference.
Related Scripture Reading: Mark 16:15–17

For Someone Who Is Dying

Lord God of Life and Death,
we commend to you your servant N.
In love you created her/him.
In love let her/him now die in peace,

and welcome her/him into the joy of your kingdom.
N., we entrust you to God who created you.
May Christ who was crucified for you
bring you freedom and peace.
May Christ who died for you
free you from every pain and suffering.
May Christ who called you
welcome you to his side.
May Christ who saved you
forgive your sins and draw you ever closer.
May Mary, the angels, and all the saints
come to meet you as you go forth from this life.
May you see your Redeemer face to face
and rejoice in the sight of God forever. Amen

*(If you are still present and the person has died, you may wish
to add the following.)*

Into your hands, Lord, we commend N.
Now that she/he has passed from this earthly life,
may she/he live on in your presence forever.
In your mercy and love,
forgive all her/his sins.
Give her/him eternal rest,
and divine consolation to all the family.
Let your light shine on all of them forever.
Amen.
Related Scripture Reading: John 14:1–3

For Someone Who Has Just Died and for the Family

Merciful God, keeper of the Book of Life,
today we have learned of the death of N.
We grieve her/his loss and absence from us,
but we thank you for our memories of her/him.
Forgive us for the missed opportunities to
love and make her/his life more enjoyable.
We trust that you are welcoming N.
into your Kingdom of Eternal Life.
Support us with your Spirit and give us the courage
to deal with N.'s absence in our life.
Be with us in our loss. Amen.
Eternal rest grant unto N., O Lord,
and may all of her/his family
receive your blessed consolation. Amen.
Related Scripture Reading: Ecclesiastes 3:1–8

Prayer of Gratitude for Restored Health or Return from Hospital

This brief service can be used for anyone who has recovered from an illness or has returned home from the hospital.

God of all gifts,
we come to you with hearts full of thanks
that N. has been restored to health
and is home again with family and friends.
In gratitude we remember the stories
of those whom Jesus healed,
of how they leaped, danced,
rejoiced, and proclaimed your glory.
It is in this spirit of joy and gratefulness
that we come to you today.
Related Scripture Reading: Mark 6:53–56

Litany of Thanks

Note: The person who was ill may wish to lead this Litany. Response after each invocation: "Thank you, Lord, for giving us life, Alleluia."

Thank you, Gracious God,
    for all the gifts you have given me.
Thank you, healing Lord,
    for rebuilding and restoring my body to health.
Thank you, healing Lord, for the marvels of medicine,
    the nurses and doctors
    who helped restore me to health.
Thank you, healing Lord,
    for all I received in my illness.
For water that cooled me, for food that sustained me,

for medication and those who treated me,
    for those who prayed and were concerned.
Thank you, healing Lord, for reuniting me
    to the flow of daily life
    and my family and neighbors.
Thank you, healing Lord,
    for the time you have allotted me,
    for the life you have offered me,
    and for the blessing of each new day.
Thank you, healing Lord, for being with me,
    for listening to me, and for taking me seriously.
Thank you, Lord, thank you very much.

Concluding Prayer

God of all gifts, you have reunited N. to the flow of
    daily life
with us, and for this we give you thanks and praise.
May she/he by proper care, rest, and recreation continue to be whole and healthy.
May she/he, and all present here,
be sensitive to those who are sick.
May we be aware of their pain
and respond to their need for support and prayer.
May our prayerful attitude
be shown in our own enjoyment of life,
in our care for others,
and in our own gift of good health.
Blessed are you, Lord our God,

who heals and saves your people.
Amen.

Part Four

Scripture Readings to Accompany Specific Prayers

For Someone Who Is Anxious or Afraid

And when Jesus got into the boat, his disciples followed him. A windstorm arose on the sea, so great that the boat was being swamped by the waves; but he was asleep. And they went and woke him up, saying, "Lord, save us! We are perishing!" And he said to them, "Why are you afraid, you of little faith?" Then he got up and rebuked the winds and the sea; and there was a dead calm. They were amazed, saying, "What sort of man is this, that even the winds and the sea obey him?" (Matthew 8:23–27).

On the Occasion of a Sudden, Unexpected Illness or Accident

For all who are led by the Spirit of God are children of God. For you did not receive a spirit of slavery to fall back into fear, but you have received a spirit of adoption. When we cry, "Abba! Father!" it is that very Spirit bearing witness with our spirit that we are children of God, and if children, then heirs, heirs of God and joint heirs with Christ—if, in fact, we suffer with him so that we may also be glorified with him. I consider that the sufferings of this present time are not worth comparing with the glory about to be revealed to us (Romans 8:14–18).

For Someone Going into Surgery

The disciples of John reported all these things to him. So John summoned two of his disciples and sent them to the Lord to ask, "Are you the one who is to come, or are we to wait for another?" Jesus had just then cured many people of diseases, plagues, and evil spirits, and had given sight to many who were blind. And he answered them, "Go and tell John what you have seen and heard: the blind receive their sight, the lame walk, the lepers are cleansed, the deaf hear, the dead are raised, the poor have good news brought to them" (Luke 7:18–22).

For Someone Recovering from Surgery

I love you Lord, because you have heard
my voice and my supplications.
Because you inclined your ear to me,
therefore I will call on you as long as I live.

The snares of death encompassed me…
I suffered distress and anguish.
Then I called on the name of the Lord:
"O Lord, I pray, save my life!"
Gracious are you Lord, and righteous;
you are merciful.
You protect the simple;
when I was brought low, you saved me.
Return, O my soul, to your rest,
for the Lord has dealt bountifully with you.
For you, O Lord, delivered my soul from death,
my eyes from tears, my feet from stumbling.
I walk before you
in the land of the living.
What shall I return to you, Lord,
for all your bounty to me?
I will lift up the cup of salvation
and call on your name (Psalm 116:1–9, 12–13).

For Someone with Cancer
Out of the depths I cry to you, O Lord.
Lord, hear my voice!
Let your ears be attentive
to the voice of my supplications!
If you, O Lord, should mark iniquities,
Lord, who could stand?

But there is forgiveness with you,
so that you may be revered.
I wait for you, Lord, my soul waits,
and in your word I hope;
my soul waits for you
more than those who watch for the morning.
O Israel, hope in the Lord!
For with you, oh Lord, there is steadfast love,
and with you is great power to redeem
(Psalm 130:1–7).

For Someone with Heart Disease

Beloved, let us love one another, because love is from God; everyone who loves is born of God and knows God. Beloved, since God loved us so much, we also ought to love one another. No one has ever seen God; if we love one another, God lives in us, and God's love is perfected in us. By this we know that we abide in God and God in us, because we have been given God's Spirit. So we have known and believe the love that God has for us. God is love, and those who love abide in God, and God abides in them (1 John 4:7, 11–13, 16).

For a Stroke Victim

May the God of peace sanctify you entirely; and may your spirit and soul and body be kept sound and blameless at the coming of our Lord Jesus Christ. The one who calls you is faithful and will do this for you (1 Thessalonians 5:23–24).

For Someone in Constant Pain

I consider that the sufferings of the present time are not worth comparing with the glory about to be revealed to us. We know that the whole creation has been groaning in labor pains until now; and not only the creation, but we ourselves, who have the first fruits of the Spirit, groan inwardly while we wait for adoption, the redemption of our bodies. For in hope we were saved. Now hope that is seen is not hope. For who hopes for what is seen? But if we hope for what we do not see, we wait for it with patience. Likewise the Spirit helps us in our weakness; for we do not know how to pray as we ought, but that very Spirit intercedes with sighs too deep for words. And God, who searches the heart knows the mind of the Spirit, because the Spirit intercedes for the saints according to the will of God (Romans 8:18, 22–27).

For Someone With a Terminal or Lingering Illness

Hear my prayer, O Lord;
let my cry come to you.
Do not hide your face from me
in the cry of my distress.
Incline your ear to me;
answer me speedily in the day when I call.
For my days pass away like smoke,
and my bones burn like a furnace.
My heart is stricken and withered like grass;
I am too wasted to eat my bread.
Because of my loud groaning
my bones cling to my skin.
I am like an owl of the wilderness,
like a little owl of the waste places.
I lie awake;
I am like a lonely bird on the housetop.
My days are like an evening shadow;
I wither away like grass.
But you, O Lord, are enthroned forever;
your name endures to all generations.
"O my God," I say, "do not take me away
at the mid-point of my life,
you whose years endure throughout all generations"
(Psalm 102:1–7, 11–12, 24).

For Someone in a Coma

Lord, you are my shepherd, I shall not want.
You make me lie down in green pastures;
you lead me beside still waters;
you restore my soul.
You lead me in right paths for your name's sake.
Even though I walk through the darkest valley,
I fear no evil;
for you are with me;
your rod and your staff—they comfort me.
You prepare a table before me
in the presence of my enemies;
you anoint my head with oil;
my cup overflows.
Surely goodness and mercy
shall follow me
all the days of my life,
and I shall dwell in the house of the Lord
my whole life long (Psalm 23).

For Sick Children

People were bringing little children to him in order
that he might touch them; and the disciples spoke
sternly to those people. But when Jesus saw this, he
was indignant and said to them, "Let the little children
come to me; do not stop them; for it is to such as these

that the kingdom of God belongs. Truly I tell you, whoever does not receive the kingdom of God as a little child will never enter it." And he took them up in his arms, laid his hands on them, and blessed them (Mark 10:13–16).

Blessing for a Premature Newborn

People were bringing even infants to him that he might touch them; and when the disciples saw it, they sternly ordered them not to do it. But Jesus called for them and said, "Let the little children come to me, and do not stop them; for it is to such as these that the kingdom of God belongs. Truly I tell you, whoever does not receive the kingdom of God as a little child will never enter it" (Luke 18:15–17).

For Someone Who Has Lost a Baby

Now the word of the Lord came to me saying,
"Before I formed you in the womb I knew you,
and before you were born I consecrated you;
I appointed you a prophet to the nations"
(Jeremiah 1:4–5).

For Someone Unable
to Receive Communion

As a deer longs for flowing streams,
so my soul longs for you, O God.
My soul thirsts for God,
for the living God.
When shall I come and behold the face of God?
My tears have been my food day and night,
while people say to me continually,
"Where is your God?"
These things I remember,
as I pour out my soul:
how I went with the throng,
and led them in procession to
the house of God,
with glad shouts and songs of thanksgiving,
a multitude keeping festival.
Why are you cast down, O my soul,
and why are you disquieted within me?
Hope in God; for I shall again offer praise
to my help and my God (Psalm 42:1–5).

For a Person Suffering from Addiction
or Substance Abuse

And Jesus said to them, "Go into all the world and pro-
claim the good news to the whole creation. The one

who believes and is baptized will be saved; but the one who does not believe will be condemned. And these signs will accompany those who believe: by using my name they will cast out demons; they will speak in new tongues" (Mark 16:15–17).

For Someone Who Is Dying

"Do not let your hearts be troubled. Believe in God, believe also in me. In my Father's house there are many dwelling places. If it were not so, would I have told you that I go to prepare a place for you? And if I go and prepare a place for you, I will come again and will take you to myself, so that where I am, there you may be also" (John 14:1–3).

For Someone Who Has Just Died and for the Family

For everything there is a season,
and a time for every matter under heaven:
a time to be born, and a time to die;
a time to plant, and a time to harvest what is planted;
a time to kill, and a time to heal;
a time to break down, and a time to build up;
a time to weep, and a time to laugh;

a time to mourn, and a time to dance;

a time to throw away stones,

and a time to gather stones together;

a time to embrace, and a time to refrain from embracing;

a time to seek, and a time to lose;

a time to keep, and a time to throw away;

a time to rip apart, and a time to repair;

a time to keep silence, and a time to speak;

a time to love, and a time to hate;

a time for war, and a time for peace

(Ecclesiastes 3:1–8).

Prayer of Gratitude for Restored Health or Return from Hospital

When they crossed over, they came to land at Genneserat and moored the boat. When they got out of the boat, people at once recognized Jesus, and rushed about that whole region and began to bring the sick on mats to wherever they heard he was. And wherever he went, into villages or cities or farms, they laid the sick in the marketplaces, and begged him that they might touch even the fringe of his cloak; and all who touched it were healed (Mark 6:53–56).

Of Related Interest. . .

Caring for Yourself When Caring for Others
Margot Hover

The author offers ways—including Scripture references, personal
stories, and prayers—for caregivers to nourish and revitalize themselves. Filled with hope, humor, and experience as a caregiver, the
author offers a very important series of reflections which should be
required reading for anyone working as a caregiver. The brief chap-
ters address the big issues in this process.

ISBN: 0-89622-533-X, 88 pp, $7.95

A Thoughtful Word, A Healing Touch
A Guide for Visiting the Sick
Joseph M. Champlin and Susan Champlin Taylor

This small booklet is a helpful resource to carry when visiting the
sick. It is filled with helpful hints and wise guidance for making
bedside visits an occasion of hope and consolation. Includes ten
pointers for visiting the sick, Scripture readings and prayers for
healing, and guidelines for praying with the sick.

ISBN: 0-89622-637-9, 40 pp, $2.95

Prayer Services for the Elderly
Giving Comfort and Joy
Sandra DeGidio, OSM

These 30 services offer ministers to the sick, both professional and
volunteer, a convenient and simple way to celebrate prayer and ritu-
al experiences in nursing homes, hospitals, and assisted care resi-
dences. They can be used with two or three people or with thirty,
depending on the situation in each facility. Clear directions and
materials needed are included in every service.

ISBN: 0-89622-685-9, 112 pp, $19.95

Available at religious bookstores or from:

 **TWENTY-THIRD PUBLICATIONS**

1-800-321-0411
E-Mail:ttpubs@aol.com